BEANS and PULSES

Susanna Miller

Illustrations by John Yates

Food

Apples
Beans and pulses
Bread
Butter
Cakes and biscuits
Cheese
Citrus fruit
Eggs
Fish
Herbs and spices
Meat
Milk
Pasta
Potatoes
Rice
Sugar
Tea
Vegetables

All words that appear in **bold** are explained in the glossary on page 30.

Editor: Fiona Corbridge

First published in 1989 by Wayland (Publishers) Limited
61 Western Road, Hove, East Sussex BN3 1JD, England.

© Copyright 1989 Wayland (Publishers) Limited

British Library Cataloguing in Publication Data
Miller, Susanna
　Beans and pulses
　1. Vegetables. Pulses
　I. Title.　II. Series
　641.3'565

ISBN 1 85210 261 6

Typeset by Kalligraphics Ltd., Horley, Surrey
Printed in Italy by G. Canale & C.S.p.A., Turin
Bound by Casterman S.A., Belgium

Contents

What are beans and pulses? 4
Beans and pulses in the past 6
The food value of pulses 8
Farming pulses 10
From harvest to shop 12
The soya bean 14
Baked beans 18
Vegetarians and vegans 20
Cooking beans and pulses 22
Things to do with pulses 24
Houmous 26
Bean salad 27
Cheesy lentil bake 28
Glossary 30
Books to read 31
Index 32

What are beans and pulses?

Beans are a type of pulse. A pulse is the edible seed of a type of pod-bearing plant, so peas and lentils are also types of pulse. Beans are a useful source of food, because they are inexpensive and highly **nutritious.**

Some beans, such as broad and runner beans, are sold fresh, but many other beans are usually dried. Dried beans take longer to cook than fresh

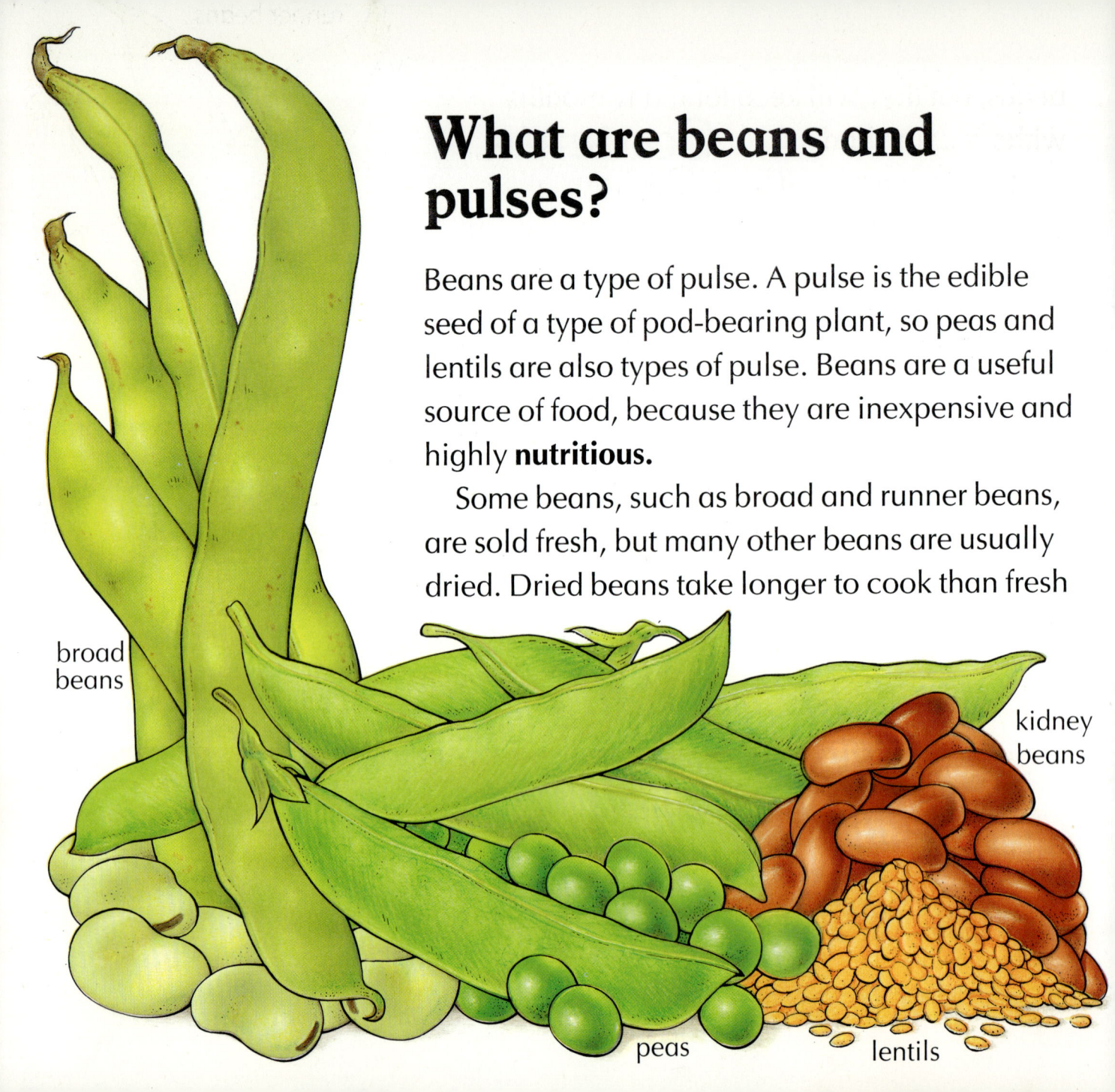

broad beans

kidney beans

peas

lentils

beans, but they will keep for many months without going bad.

There is one type of bean which you will almost certainly have eaten: the haricot bean. Baked beans are haricot beans, which we buy in cans in a tasty tomato sauce. Other popular types of bean include red kidney beans, aduki beans, mung beans and soya beans. Soya beans are special because they contain so much **protein** – nearly twice as much as chicken and three times as much as beef.

Beans and pulses in the past

Pulses were one of the very first crops to be **cultivated** by people. Peas found in Thailand have been proved to date back to 9750 BC, and others found in Hungary and Switzerland date back to the Bronze Age (about 3000 BC). The ancient Egyptians, Greeks and Romans all

A crop of soya beans drying on a Chinese farm. Soya beans were first grown in China, 5,000 years ago.

cultivated various pulses. We also know that the ancient Hebrews ate pulses, for they are mentioned several times in the Bible.

As well as being a food, pulses have had other uses. The ancient Greeks and Romans used beans for casting their votes in elections. In ancient Egypt, beans were at one time considered a symbol of life, although at another time they were believed to contain the souls of the dead. In medieval times, beans were used in medicines and **sorcery.**

These Egyptian women are sifting lentils in preparation for a feast. Pulses have been cultivated in Egypt since ancient times.

The food value of pulses

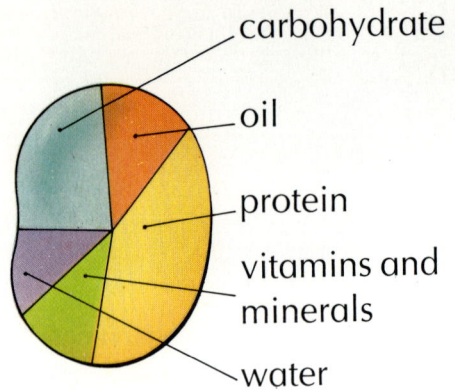

Above *This diagram shows the different amounts of nutrients in a soya bean. Soya beans contain more protein than any other bean.*

Pulses are high in fibre and protein, and low in sugar and fat. This means they are very good for a healthy diet.

Fibre helps our digestive systems to work properly. Protein builds new cells and repairs damaged tissues. Different groups of foods contain different types of protein, and our bodies get the best nutritional value when we eat

Right *A meal of beans on toast provides our bodies with both pulse and cereal proteins.*

A market stall in Ankara, Turkey, selling pulses, dried fruit and seeds.

different types. For example, beans on toast combines pulse and cereal proteins.

Too much sugar and fat are bad for us. They can make us overweight and cause illnesses such as heart disease.

Vitamins and minerals are **substances** found in small quantities in food. Our bodies need them only in tiny amounts, but without them we would suffer from diseases. Pulses contain important vitamins and minerals such as vitamin B, iron and phosphorus.

Farming pulses

Pulses belong to the family of plants called *leguminosae*. There are about 14,000 species of *leguminosae*, which grow nearly all over the world. Pulses like a warm, **temperate** climate.

The USA is one of the world's largest exporters of pulses. Britain buys haricot beans from the USA for the 900 million cans of baked beans eaten every year. The world's largest producer of

Watering a crop of snowpeas in Thailand.

Inspecting soya bean seedlings on a farm in Brazil.

lentils is India. The USA, Argentina, Egypt, Ethiopia, Morocco, Spain, Syria and Turkey also grow a lot of lentils.

Pulses take about three months to grow. At harvesting time, the plants are cut and left to dry. Mechanical harvesters then gather up the plants and pass them through **threshing** cylinders to separate the pods, containing the pulses, from the waste part of the plant. In very dry areas, plants may be left to dry out before they are harvested.

From harvest to shop

After harvesting, the pods are taken to a processing plant, where a machine removes the pulses and discards the pods. The pulses are washed, and may then be graded into different sizes. This is done by passing the pulses over wire mesh, through which the smaller seeds fall.

Some pulses undergo special preparation. For example, to make split peas, the peas are first soaked and steamed to soften their outer skin.

Harvesting beans by hand on a farm near Faro, Portugal.

Using a combine harvester to harvest soya beans in Louisiana, USA.

They are then put into a machine called a splitter, which hurls the peas against metal plates to make them split in half. After this they are graded and polished to make them look attractively shiny.

Pulses are usually sold ready packaged, but some health food shops keep big sacks of pulses from which they weigh out what you want. Some pulses are prepared and sold in tins ready for immediate use. This is very convenient, but more expensive than buying dried pulses.

The soya bean

Soya beans are one of the oldest vegetables known to us. They were first grown 5,000 years ago, in China. The soya bean is a small, round, golden-beige coloured bean, which needs to be soaked for several hours and then cooked for several more before it can be eaten.

Protein is a very important food, which our bodies need to build new cells and keep healthy.

Above Harvesting soya in South Dakota, USA. The USA grows over 60 per cent of the world's supply of soya.

Opposite Farming soya in Zaire.

Soya beans contain more protein than any other pulse. Protein is made up of hundreds of **amino acids,** eight of which are essential to us. The soya bean contains all eight of these amino acids.

In the West, we get most of our protein from animals, in the form of meat, fish, eggs and milk. In poorer countries, people often do not get enough of these foods to eat. Soya is cheap, easy to grow, and rich in protein, so it is an excellent alternative. Many scientists believe that soya could help solve the problem of feeding the millions of people in the world who are starving.

The USA grows over 60 per cent of the world's supply of soya. Brazil and China also produce large amounts.

Soya beans are made into many products, such as flour, oil, margarine and milk. Soya beans are also made into textured vegetable protein (TVP). Soya flour is mixed with water and

Many scientists believe that soya could help with the problem of feeding the world's starving millions.

These 'meat flavour' foods are made from TVP, a soya product.

cooked. A machine called an extruder forms the mixture into chunks, granules or other shapes. The mixture can even be flavoured to taste like meat! TVP is used in many different food products.

Soya bean meal is used as an important protein-rich feed for livestock and poultry. Soya also has hundreds of industrial uses. For example, it is used to make paint, glue, paper, plastics, **insecticides** and explosives.

Baked beans

The American firm of H. J. Heinz first produced baked beans with tomato sauce in 1895.

Baked beans are a very popular and nutritious food. Thousands of millions of cans of beans are eaten every year. Baked beans are a type of haricot bean called 'navy' beans. They are actually white, but when we buy them as baked beans, they are in a tomato sauce.

This is how baked beans are made. The harvested dry beans are graded, sorted and cleaned. The beans are then soaked in hot water to soften them. This is called blanching. Next, the beans are baked and put into cans with the special tomato sauce. The lids are then sealed on. The cans pass through a machine which cooks the beans at a very high temperature by steam. This destroys any **bacteria** that may be present. It then cools the cans with water, and dries them ready for labelling.

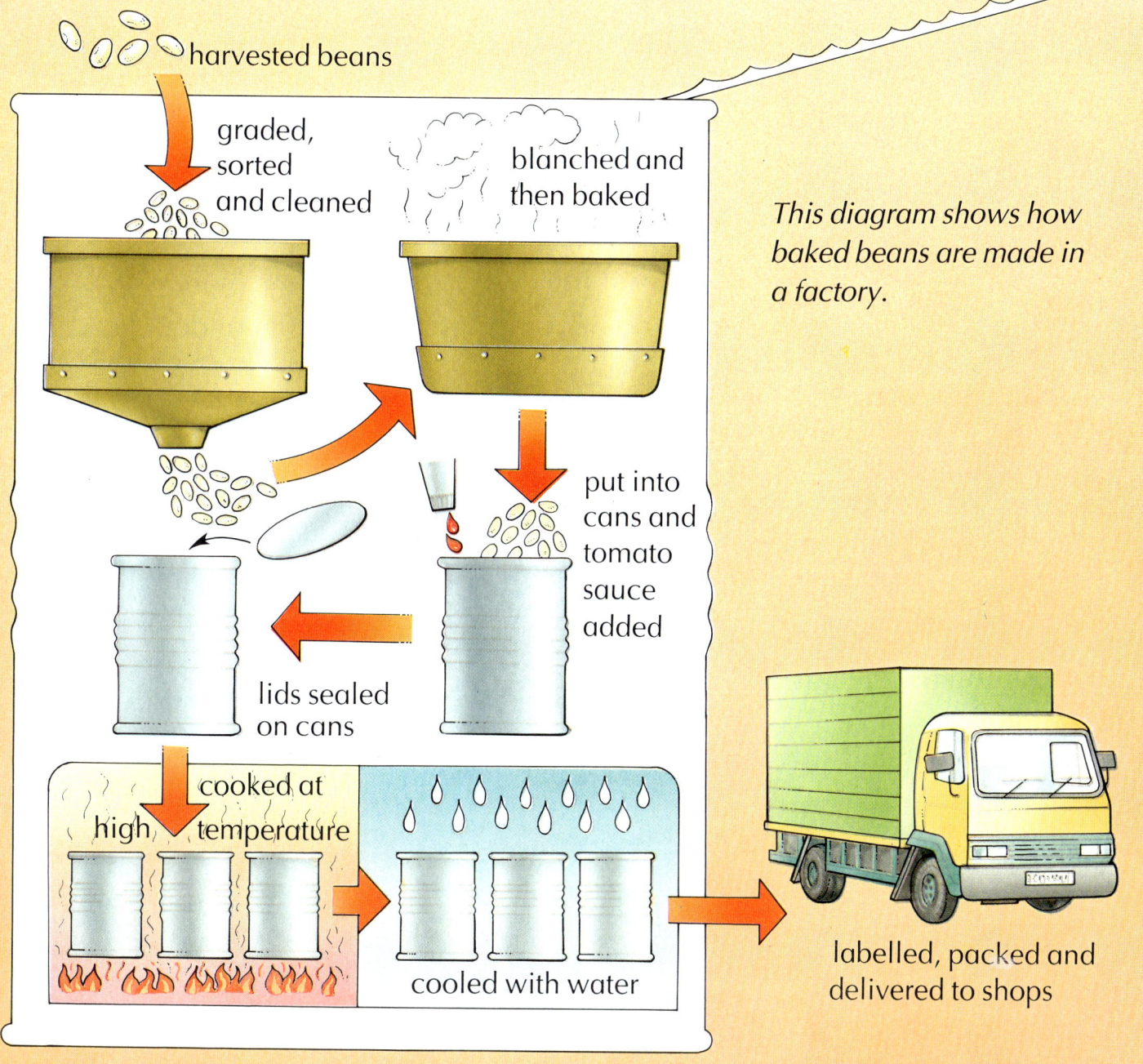

Vegetarians and vegans

Because they are high in protein, pulses are particularly important in the diet of people who do not eat meat. Such people are called vegetarians or vegans. Vegetarians do not eat meat, poultry or fish, nor do they eat products which involve the slaughter of animals, such as **gelatine** and lard. Vegetarians do eat dairy products. Vegans do not eat any meat or animal

Above *Choosing vegetables in a Chinese supermarket.*

Above *These Buddhist monks are enjoying a vegetarian meal at a temple in Thailand.*

Opposite *These tasty vegetarian dishes are prepared without meat. Many people consider that a vegetarian diet is healthier than one containing meat.*

products, not even dairy produce. Some vegans do not eat honey, because they believe that living creatures should not be used for any sort of farming.

There are many reasons for being vegetarian. Some religions, such as Buddhism and Hinduism, forbid their followers to eat meat. Some people believe that killing animals for food is wrong, and that modern farming methods cause animals unnecessary suffering. Other people consider a vegetarian diet to be more healthy than one containing meat.

Cooking beans and pulses

Lentils, split peas and tinned pulses can be cooked without any preparation, but dried beans and peas must be soaked for several hours before cooking. It is important to use plenty of water for soaking, because pulses will absorb twice their own weight in water. A quicker method is to cover the pulses with boiling water, leave for ten

Above *Pulses must be soaked before they are cooked.*

Right *Tofu, or beancurd, is made from soya beans and is used in many recipes. Here it is being prepared in a factory in Tokyo, Japan.*

Opposite *A burger made from soya beans, served with vegetables, makes a satisfying meal.*

minutes, drain and pour over fresh boiling water. They will be ready in an hour.

Recipes will tell you how long it takes to cook different pulses. Lentils cook in about twenty minutes, but larger beans need about an hour. Red kidney beans must be boiled for fifteen minutes, then drained, put in fresh water and the cooking continued. This boiling is needed to destroy a harmful **enzyme** contained in the skin of the bean. And remember to add salt to pulses at the end of cooking: if you add it earlier it will make their skins tough.

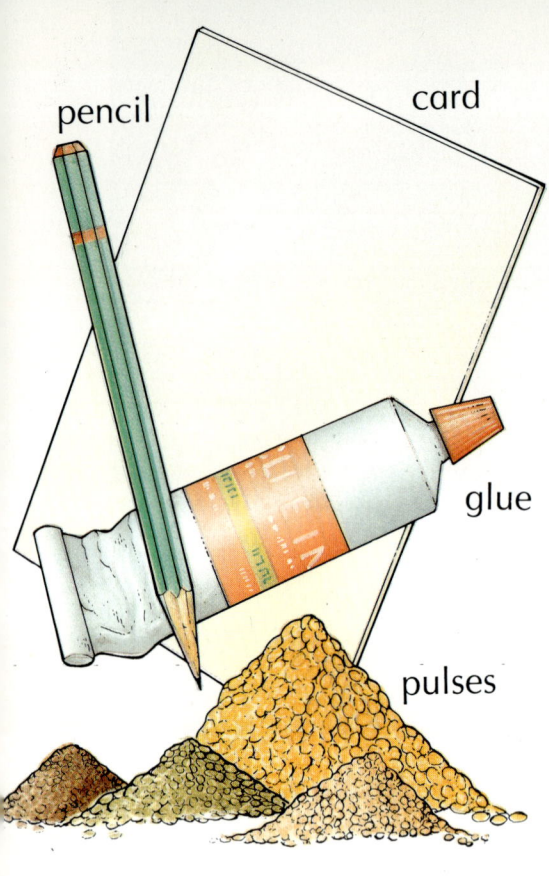

Things to do with pulses

Make a mosaic picture

You will need: card or strong paper, a pencil or pen, glue, a selection of pulses.

Draw your design on the card or paper: perhaps a pattern, a face or a design of your name. Then use the pulses to fill in your design. To do this, spread the glue over a little of your design at a time, and fill in your picture with different pulses. For example, little red and yellow split peas are good for hair, larger beans for eyes or a nose.

1.   2.   3.   4.

Grow your own beansprouts to eat

You will need: mung beans or whole lentils, a jam jar, a piece of muslin, an elastic band. Place two tablespoons of beans in the jam jar, cover with cold water and leave for eight to twelve hours. Cover the jar with the muslin and fasten with the elastic band. Drain the water through the muslin, refill the jar with fresh water and drain again. Keep the jar in the airing-cupboard and rinse and drain twice a day for a few days, until small shoots have grown.

Houmous

This is a creamy dip, popular throughout the Middle East. Traditionally, it is served with pitta bread, but crusty bread or raw vegetables also go well with it.

You will need, for 4 people:
225g chick peas
4 teaspoons tahini (from a health food shop)
2 crushed garlic cloves
2 tablespoons lemon juice
salt and freshly ground black pepper
6–8 tablespoons olive oil

1. Soak and cook the chick peas. Drain them, keeping 120 ml of the cooking liquid.

2. Put the chick peas, cooking liquid, tahini, garlic, olive oil and lemon juice into a blender (be sure to get a grown-up to help you). Blend until smooth, then season with salt and pepper.

3. Spoon the houmous into a serving dish and pour a little olive oil over the top before serving. Decorate it with lemon slices or olives if you like.

Bean salad

You will need:
75g red kidney beans
75g haricot beans
100g fresh French beans
6 tablespoons olive oil
2 tablespoons wine or cider vinegar
½ teaspoon dry mustard
½ teaspoon caster sugar
2–3 tablespoons chopped fresh herbs
  e.g. parsley, mint, chives
salt and freshly ground black pepper

2. Cut the French beans into 1cm lengths and boil them in a little water for about 3 minutes, until just tender.

3. Put the oil, vinegar, mustard and sugar into a clean screw-top jar and shake until blended.

1. Soak and cook the red kidney beans and haricot beans separately (if you cook them together the kidney beans will turn the haricot beans pink!).

4. Mix the beans together in a bowl and pour the dressing over. Doing this when the beans are still warm will help the flavours to blend. Add the herbs, salt and pepper to taste, and mix gently. Serve the salad chilled.

Cheesy lentil bake

You will need, for 4 people:
225g split red lentils
100g grated cheddar cheese
1 medium-sized onion
2 tomatoes
450ml water
salt and freshly ground pepper
a little butter or margarine
½ teaspoon dried oregano or
    marjoram

1. Chop the onion and slice the tomatoes (get a grown-up to help you).

2. Put the chopped onion and lentils into a saucepan with the water, bring to the boil and simmer gently for about 20 minutes until the water is absorbed and the lentils are tender.

3. Mix in half the cheese and the oregano (or marjoram), and season with salt and pepper.

4. Press the mixture into a greased loaf tin or 18–20 cm square tin.

5. Arrange the tomato slices over the top and sprinkle with the rest of the grated cheese. Dot the top with a little butter or margarine. Bake in an oven heated to 200°C/400°F/gas mark 6 for 25–30 minutes until the top is golden and crunchy.

6. Serve this crispy bake in slices with salad or potatoes and vegetables.

Glossary

Amino acids Any of a group of substances found in foods. Proteins are made up of them.
Bacteria Tiny living organisms present in the air which, when they settle on food, increase in number very quickly. Eventually they destroy the food, usually making it harmful to eat.
Cultivated Plants specially grown and cared for by people.
Enzymes Substances formed by the cells of plants and animals, some of which may be harmful to us.
Gelatine A substance made from animal bones and muscles, which is used to set foods such as jellies and mousses.
Insecticides Preparations used for killing insects.
Nutritious Food which is healthy and good for you.
Protein Substances in food which help the body to grow and to mend itself.
Sorcery The practice of magic by casting spells.
Substances Materials or matter which make up an object.
Temperate A climate which is moderate and mild.

Threshing Beating the stalks of a ripe crop in order to separate the pods or grain from the rest of the plant. This may be done by using a hand implement or by machine.

Books to read

Health and Food by Dorothy Baldwin (Wayland, 1987)
Favourite Food: Baked Beans by Chris Evans (Studio Vista, 1975)
Focus on Soya by Susan Goddard (Wayland, 1986)
You and Your Food by Judy Tatchell and Dilys Wells (Usborne, 1985)

Index

Animal feed 17
Argentina 11

Beans
  aduki 5
  baked 5, 8, 9, 10, 18–19
  broad 4
  butter 5
  haricot 5, 10, 18, 27
  kidney 5, 23, 27
  mung 5, 25
  runner 4
  soya 5, 6, 8, 11, 13, 14–17, 22, 23
Brazil 11, 16
Britain 10, 18
Buddhism 21

Chick peas 5, 26
China 6, 14, 16, 19
Cooking 14, 18, 19, 22–3

Drying 4, 5, 11, 13, 22

Egypt 4, 5, 7, 11
Ethiopia 11

Farming 10–11, 14, 21
Fibre 8

Grading 12, 13, 18, 19

Harvesting 11, 12, 13, 15, 18, 19
Hindus 21
Hungary 6

India 11
Insecticides 17

Japan 23

Lentils 4, 7, 11, 22, 23, 25, 28–9

Markets 9
Morocco 11

Paint 17
Peas 4, 6, 12, 13, 22

Pods 4, 11, 12
Portugal 12
Processing 12–13, 18, 19
Protein 5, 8, 9, 14, 15, 20

Shops 13, 19
Sorcery 7
Spain 11
Switzerland 6
Syria 11

Thailand 6, 10, 21
Threshing 11
Tofu 23
Turkey 9, 11
TVP 16, 17

USA 10, 11, 13, 15, 16, 18

Vegans 20–21
Vegetarians 20–21
Vitamins and minerals 9

Zaire 14

Picture acknowledgements

The photographs in this book were provided by: J. Allan Cash 6, 11, 12, 22; H. J. Heinz Company 8, 18; Holt Studios 10, 13; The Hutchison Library 9, 14, 15, 16, 21; Christine Osborne 7, 20; Wayland Picture Library 17; Zefa 23.